May, 2004
To the Weiss Boys—

Seymour Simon

Spiders

SEYMOUR SIMON

HarperCollins*Publishers*

Most of us have seen a spider or a spiderweb at home or outdoors. Spiders live nearly everywhere around the world—in grasslands, forests, mountains, deserts, ponds, schools, and houses, and on ocean-going ships.

About 35,000 different kinds of spiders have been identified and named. Scientists think that there are at least that many more kinds of spiders yet to be discovered.

Spiders are not the most popular kind of animal. Some people scream or run away from them. They think spiders are ugly and poisonous. Actually, only a very few are poisonous to people. Each year, far more people get sick or die from bee stings or other insect bites than from spider bites.

Spiders do much more good than harm. They eat insects that damage crops and other plants. Scientists wish to learn more about the way spiders spin silk and the unique properties of spider silk. Some spiders even make interesting pets.

If you take the time to look at spiders in nature and read about them, you may be surprised to learn just how fascinating they are.

Spiders come in many different sizes and colors. Some spiders are as small as the period at the end of this sentence. Other spiders, such as tarantulas, are huge. They are as big as your hand and large enough to catch and eat birds. Many male spiders are much smaller than female spiders.

The colors and shapes of some spiders help them blend in with the ground and make them difficult to spot. Many spiders are a dull brown or gray color, which makes them almost invisible on the ground. Other spiders are yellow, red, or orange. These spiders may taste bad, and the bright colors warn enemies to leave them alone.

Some spiders have short, fat bodies with hairy legs. Others are thin with long, skinny legs. There are spiders that look like flowers and spiders that look like grapes. There are spiders with horns and spiders with spines. Some spiders even look like bird droppings!

What is a spider? A spider has two main body parts, the head and the abdomen. The head has eyes and a mouth but no ears or nose. It contains the brain, the stomach, and poison glands. The abdomen, the back part of the spider, contains the heart, lungs, silk glands, and reproductive organs.

Here's how to tell spiders apart from insects. All spiders have two body parts and eight legs. All insects have three body parts, six legs, and antennae. Some insects have wings. No spiders have wings or antennae. Some insects make silk but not the way spiders make silk. So spiders are not insects. They are related to mites, ticks, and scorpions.

What do spiders and insects have in common? They have a hard outer skeleton and legs with jointed sections.

A spider's skin is like a suit of armor. It is made of a stiff material called chitin. Chitin can't stretch the way your skin does. As a spider grows, it sheds its skin and grows a new one.

Two large jaws stick out of a spider's mouth. A curved fang is at the tip of each jaw. Each fang is attached to a poison sac. Alongside a spider's jaws are pedipalps, appendages used as feelers and to hold down prey.

Most spiders have eight eyes. They are placed in two or three rows on the spider's head. The main eyes are the middle pair of eyes in the first row. They can focus and produce an image the way a camera lens does. The smaller eyes are light sensitive. They can pick up movement from a distance and help the spider sense danger from birds and other animals that eat spiders.

Jumping spiders, wolf spiders, and most hunting spiders have large main eyes. They can see clearly over a small area that is a few inches away. This helps the spider find prey and pounce when it gets close enough.

Despite all their eyes, spiders have poor eyesight. They rely on their sense of touch rather than vision. Sensitive hairs cover their body and legs. The hairs send signals to the brain, alerting the spider to movement around it. Orb-weaving spiders use special slits on their bodies to detect vibrations of struggling insects trapped in their webs.

There are two main types of spiders: web builders and hunting or wandering spiders. Web builders use their webs to trap flying insects. Hunting spiders wander along the ground and catch crawling insects. Each type of spider has a body that is best for the way it moves and hunts.

Spiders can run, jump, climb on smooth surfaces, and hang upside down. They can move quickly but can't keep it up for very long. Web builders have a special claw at the end of each leg to help them hold on to the silk in their webs.

Many kinds of hunting spiders have tufts of hair between their claws at the end of their legs. The hairs pull up some of the moisture on objects and seem to glue the spider's leg to smooth surfaces, even a glass pane.

All spiders can make silk. They use it to make webs, traps, burrows, and cocoons. Some spider silk is three times stronger than a steel wire of the same thickness. Spider silk can be thinner than a human hair and can stretch to twice its length.

Spiders make up to seven kinds of silk with glands in their abdomen. Each kind of silk is used in a particular way, such as making traps, wrapping up prey, or providing shelter. Female spiders make a kind of silk to encase and protect their eggs.

Spinnerets are tiny tubes near the end of a spider's body. Silk comes out of the spinnerets as a liquid. Then, the spider pulls on the silk and it hardens into a thread.

Spiders use a double thread of silk to make a dragline that trails behind them. Spiders use the dragline to get back home quickly or to drop out of sight until a threat passes.

Five thousand kinds of spiders build orb-shaped or circular webs. A common garden spider uses from 50 to 200 feet of silk to build an orb-shaped web about a foot across in less than an hour. An orb-web spider spins about 100 webs during its lifetime.

To start its web, an orb weaver lets out a silky thread across an open space. Wind carries the thread until it catches on a spot on a distant tree or bush. The spider pulls the thread tight and marches across the silky bridge. Hanging from the bridge line, the spider builds a frame for its web. Silky spokes stretch from the center, or hub, like the spokes of a bicycle wheel.

The spider returns to the hub. Next, it weaves a dry spiral web to strengthen the spokes and hold them in place. Now starting from the outside, the spider spins another spiral of sticky silk going back inward, toward the hub.

When the web is finished, the spider waits for insects to fly into its web. An orb web is thin and difficult to see, yet it is strong enough to hold flying or jumping insects. When the spider feels the web vibrating, it knows that an insect is caught. The spider rushes in for the kill.

Spiders build webs and traps in many shapes and sizes besides orbs. Purse-web spiders live inside tubes of tightly woven silk alongside a tree trunk or well hidden in the grass. The purse is about a foot and a half long and about as thick as your finger. When an insect walks over the purse, the spider spears it with sharp fangs and pulls it inside.

Funnel-weaving spiders build webs in the grass that look like funnels. The spider hides in the small end and waits for an insect to wander into the opening of the large end of the funnel.

Some spiders use silk to capture insects in unusual ways. Net-casting spiders throw strong, silky webs over their prey. A bolas spider throws a ball of sticky silk attached to the end of a long silk line at an insect the way a cowboy might lasso cattle. The insect sticks to the ball and the spider pulls it in. A spitting spider spits out sticky poisonous silk over an insect that wanders by. Then the spider bites down!

Some spiders don't wait around for their prey. They don't build webs or traps. A hunting or wandering spider catches prey the way a tiger stalks a deer or a cat stalks a mouse. The spider follows its prey along the ground. When it is within range, the spider leaps on and grabs the prey with its powerful jaws.

Spiders are not picky about what they eat. They go after beetles, grasshoppers, bees, and other insects. Bigger spiders may catch small animals such as fish, mice, and birds. Spiders even eat other spiders. In a spider's world, it's eat or be eaten!

Jumping spiders are champion jumpers that always make their target. A jumping spider can leap a distance about 40 times the length of its own body. That would be like you jumping the length of two basketball courts and making a slam dunk.

Nearly all spiders use poison to paralyze their prey and as a defense against their enemies. Spider poison, called venom, is injected into the prey through the spider's fangs. It can kill an insect or other small prey. Only a few kinds of spiders, such as the female black widow, make nerve venom that is powerful enough to kill a person.

This shy spider hides in dark places and runs away if disturbed. Sometimes she hides inside a shoe or inside clothing and gets pressed against a person's bare skin. She bites to protect herself. A black widow's bite is about 15 times more poisonous than that of a rattlesnake. It causes paralysis and may cause death. Fortunately, an antidote can be given to save a person's life.

Widow spiders are named for the female's behavior of eating the male after mating. All black widows have an hourglass red mark on the underside of the abdomen.

Another dangerous spider is the brown recluse. Bites from recluse spiders can cause ulcers that destroy skin tissue and sometimes even cause death.

Tarantulas are the largest spiders in the world. Their hairy bodies and huge fangs look dangerous. But tarantulas are not as dangerous as they look. Due to their small poison glands, their bite is about as painful as a hornet or bee sting. Some kinds of Mexican tarantulas have become popular pets.

In most spiders, the jaws open and close like a pair of pliers. But in tarantulas, the jaws move up and down. During a confrontation with a nesting bird or a tree frog, a tarantula raises its front legs, lifts its head, and exposes its fangs. When it bites, a tarantula stabs downward, pointing its fangs like two daggers.

Most spiders live only about a year, but female tarantulas may live for more than 20 years. The males are not so lucky. They may be eaten by the females after mating.

Spiders don't live in the ocean, but several kinds of spiders live in and around freshwater ponds and lakes and slow-moving streams. Fishing spiders spend their lives floating on leaves or twigs. They eat small fish, tadpoles, and insects that have fallen into the water. Ripples alert the spider to the distance and location of its prey.

One type of water spider that lives in Europe and Asia spends much of its life underwater inside an air bubble called a diving bell. To make a diving bell, the spider spins a web attached to an underwater plant. Then it swims to the surface, traps a bubble of air, and carries the bubble down to its web. A water spider eats, mates, and lays its eggs inside the bell.

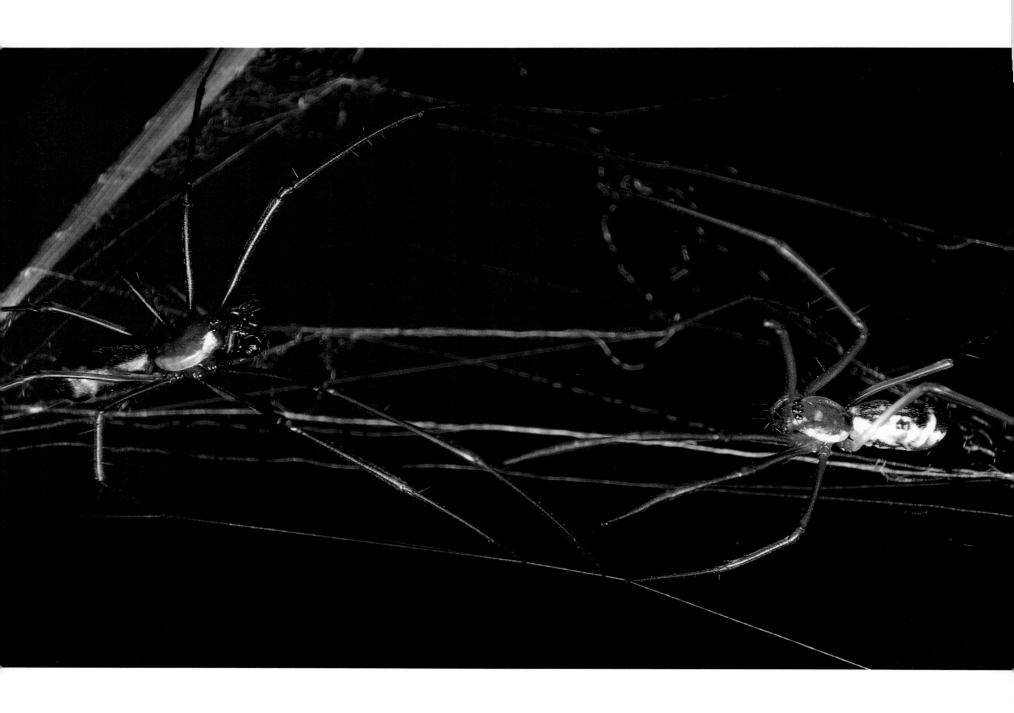

When they are ready to mate, female spiders attract male spiders by giving off a scent or odor that is specific to their kind. Once a male finds a female, he signals so that she won't mistake him for a meal wandering by. A male wolf spider waves his pedipalps like signal flags when he spots a female. Male jumping spiders twist and twirl to attract a female.

Orb-weaving spiders have poor eyesight, so the males use other methods. Some tug on the female's web. A male nursery web spider wraps up a gift of insect food in a silk package and presents it to the female.

All female spiders lay eggs, usually a week or two after mating. Depending upon the size of the female, she may lay from one to more than 1,000 eggs at a time. As the eggs are laid, they are fertilized with the male's sperm. The outer part of the egg hardens, and the female spins a cocoon of silk around the eggs to protect them. Some spiders cover the cocoon with plant parts, insect bodies, and dirt. Others hide the eggs under rocks or underneath the bark of a tree. Some female spiders carry their eggs around with them until they hatch.

A female wolf spider carries her egg case on her back for about a week. Then she cuts open the egg case and the babies hatch. For several days, the baby spiders, called spiderlings, get a piggyback ride from their mother.

When they are born, spiderlings look like tiny models of their parents. They grow up quickly and need to find food soon. Many spiderlings spin threads of silk that are caught by the wind. They are carried to new places to live and grow. This is called ballooning.

You can find spiders just about anywhere. They are inside your house or in the backyard. They are in a meadow or a city park. See if you can find spiderwebs or wandering spiders. You may find a jumping spider hunting for prey on the ground alongside rocks or logs.

Spiders can look pretty scary with their eight hairy legs and all those eyes. Some people are really afraid of them. You should never touch a spider if you aren't sure what kind it is. But most of us can become less frightened of spiders just by watching and learning more about them.

For Joel, Benjamin, Chloe, and Jeremy
—From Grandpa, with love

Photos do not reflect actual size of spiders.

PHOTO CREDITS: title page © Robert Lubeck / Animals Animals; p. 2 © Ross Frid 1996 / Visuals Unlimited; p. 4, p. 5 (TOP RIGHT), p. 11, p. 21, p. 26, p. 32 © James H. Robinson; p. 5 (TOP LEFT) © Richard Shiell / Animals Animals, p. 5 (BOTTOM LEFT) © Paul Freed / Animals Animals; p. 6 © Steven David Miller / Animals Animals; p. 7, p. 12 © Kjell B. Sandved / Visuals Unlimited; p. 9 © Gary Gaugler / Visuals Unlimited; p. 10, p. 27 © W.F. Mantis / Animals Animals; p. 13 © Renee Andrews / Visuals Unlimited; p. 14, p. 15 © James H. Robinson / Animals Animals; p. 16 © Bill Beatty / Animals Animals; p. 17, p. 29 © Bill Beatty / Visuals Unlimited; p. 18 © Stephen Dalton / Animals Animals; p. 22 © G and C Merker / Visuals Unlimited; p. 23 © Richard La Val / Animals Animals; p. 24 © Oxford Scientific Films / Animals Animals; p. 25 © H.L. Fox / Animals Animals; p. 28 © James E. Gerholdt; p. 30 © Scott W. Smith / Animals Animals; p. 31 © Bruce Davidson / Animals Animals

Special thanks to William Holmstrom, Collection Manager, Department of Herpetology, Wildlife Conservation Society, for his expert advice.

Library of Congress Cataloging-in-Publication Data
Simon, Seymour.
Spiders / by Seymour Simon—1st ed.
p.   cm.
Summary: An introduction to the physical characteristics, behavior, and life cycle of different kinds of spiders.
ISBN 0-06-028391-2 —ISBN 0-06-028392-0 (lib. bdg.)
1. Spiders—Juvenile literature.   [1. Spiders.]   1. Title.
QL458.4 .S585   2003   2002014922   595.4'4—dc21

Typography by Al Cetta   1 2 3 4 5 6 7 8 9 10   ❖   First Edition